ENSURING A BETTER FUTURE

WHY SOCIAL STUDIES MATTERS

29 28 27 26 25 24 23 22   1 2 3 4 5

Published by Gibbs Smith Education
P.O. Box 667
Layton, UT 84041
801.544.9800
www.gibbssmitheducation.com

Publisher: Jared L. Taylor
Editorial Director: Elizabeth Wallace
Managing Editor: Michelle DeVries
Author: Dr. Kevin Colleary
Editor: Giacomo J. Calabria
Cover design: Dennis Wunsch
Photo Editor: Anna-Morgan Leonards
Copyeditor: Heather Kerrigan

Gibbs Smith books are printed on either recycled, 100% post-consumer
waste, FSC-certified papers, or on paper produced from a 100%
certified sustainable forest/controlled wood source.

Printed and bound in the U.S.A.
ISBN: 978-1-4236-5799-6

CONTENTS

INTRODUCTION

"Thanks, Professor," one of my graduate students—a third-grade teacher in the South Bronx—said after a particularly interesting and invigorating class discussion on the importance of teaching history and social studies. "Great ideas and information. Too bad I don't ever get to use any of it at my school." She shrugged and left the room.

I have thought many times about the students in that teacher's class, and the classes in schools throughout the nation, who have suffered due to our lack of or reduced instruction in history, geography, economics, and civics. The narrowing of the curriculum and the dilution of students' experiences with content instruction has been a simmering problem for at least 20 years (Jerald, 2006). Over 44 percent of US public school districts in one survey responded that they had specifically reduced instructional time for social studies in their elementary school curricula since the introduction of No Child Left Behind (Fitchett et al., 2014). Studies report the average time spent on social studies in US K–3 classrooms is 16 minutes per week (Banilower et al., 2013). In my own teaching, I ask graduate students, all elementary school teachers in New York, about their experiences. The following are some of their responses:

> "No curriculum except English/language arts and math."
> "No specific social studies teaching time."
> "Thirty minutes per week, often taken over by specials."
> "We have social studies and science blocks, but I'm often told to use the time to get to English/language arts standards." (Colleary, 2018)

Watching social studies fall off the curricular table has been a painful reality. But it has been seemingly accepted by our profession, communities, and nation. Pace (2012) reported that "[t]he apparent mainstream acceptance of drastic reductions in the amount of time and attention given to elementary education's core academic subjects is shocking" (p. 353). As the Educating for American Democracy Initiative ("About Us," 2021) reports, "At the federal level, we spend approximately $50 per student per year on STEM fields and approximately $0.05 per student per year on civics." This is a striking data point that sadly supports the research-based and anecdotal evidence mentioned above. In addition, we have seen a recent assault on the teaching of certain aspects of history at all levels in a majority of US states. In many places, organized and usually politically motivated legislative or policy efforts have been introduced or enacted to restrict education on racism, bias, the contributions of specific racial or ethnic groups to US history, or related topics (Harris, 2021; Stout & LeMee, 2021).

In this book, I will present arguments and perspectives on why the multifaceted challenges regarding social studies education in the United States pose such a threat and why fighting to resolve problems and restore the place of social studies education can help ensure our future. While the problem is not new, we are approaching a tipping point in our nation's history, a precipice from which we may no longer step back. In 2017, 35 percent of millennials said they were losing faith in American democracy, and just 25 percent were confident in the democratic system (CIRCLE, 2017). Scholars, journalists, and political scientists are writing more often and more directly about the rise of autocracy, collapse of democratic societies, and even the possibility of another US civil war (Applebaum, 2020;

Coleman, 2022; Meachem, 2021; Walter, 2022). These challenges are bigger than any one academic discipline can change. However, the connections between what we do or do not teach children and how our society develops are real. It is the purpose of education.

In the Irish immigrant home in which I grew up, education was highly valued. While intelligent people, neither of my parents had gone to high school, and so they knew little of formal education processes or patterns, especially in the United States. Anything we needed to know about school, and certainly everything presented to us in school, we had to process and understand ourselves. Most working-class immigrant children understand this reality. While your parents love, feed, protect, and take care of you as best they can, they are often limited in how much they can help you navigate the world. Perhaps this played a role in why social studies spoke to me as a young student. The concepts and questions of history, geography, civics, and economics, and the fascinating details about people, places, what happened, when, how, and why, were always intriguing to me. I needed to know and understand how this world worked in ways that my parents couldn't teach me. Perhaps it was about finding one's place in the larger picture and, as a working-class kid with foreign-born parents, wanting to know as much as I could about what that place might eventually be. I also believe, however, that my love of social studies content and learning was prompted by the teachers I was lucky enough to know and learn from. I received not only a solid basic education but also an even greater gift: the love of learning about the world. I learned that I belonged to a community of citizens and learned to love my country and its promise. There was also much that I did not learn. As a white student in a predominantly white community, there was no discussion of systemic racism or white privilege. While there were lessons about Malcolm X, Rosa Parks, Dr. Martin Luther King Jr., and the Civil Rights Movement, we never learned about the redlining and other pervasive racist practices that happened in our community to keep African Americans and other nonwhite families out (Hannah-Jones, 2012). While most of my teachers were strong, well-educated women, we did not regularly discuss gender inequities or how the patriarchy affected so many elements of our lives. Sexual diversity was also a taboo topic and never discussed during my K–12 education, even in sex education classes. By the upper elementary grades, we knew enough, however, to understand that if anyone may have had a sexually diverse identity, it was not to be discussed openly or positively. I look back on my education with gratitude but also with regret for all that was hidden, silenced, and covered up. I think about how much richer and more honest my understanding of the world could have been if I was given access to these realities in addition to the beneficial, but limited, education I did receive.

In *Ensuring the Future: Why Social Studies Matters*, I hope to record some of these observations and present arguments for how we might fix a dangerous, simmering problem. The phrase "ensuring the future" was carefully selected. This book is being written at a critical juncture in US and world history. On one hand, we have seen a distinct rise in support for authoritarian leaders and populist governments around the world (Applebaum, 2018), a continuous growth in the "civic achievement gap" among socioeconomic groups (Levinson, 2007), growing inequity in society at large (Organization for Economic Co-operation and Development, 2021), and declining levels of positive beliefs among young people in the benefits of democratic forms of government (Ladd et al. 2018). We have also seen the recent unprovoked attacks in Ukraine by the autocratic government of the Russian Federation, which some see as a war not just on a sovereign nation but also on the broader concepts of democracy and an open society (McCance,

2022). On the other hand, we are experiencing a renewal of interest in critical issues of gender equity, power structure, racial privilege, and deep-seated structural inequities. Many young people are becoming involved in growing calls for critical examination and change of current societal structures. We have recently experienced a once-in-a-lifetime health crisis and global pandemic that has left no one unscathed. Millions are dead around the world, hundreds of thousands of families have been shattered, communities are torn apart, and it is still too soon to truly understand the full impact on education, health care, work, and family life. Our local communities, nation, profession, and world are asking questions and posing problems that demand attention. I write this book as an argument, defense of a position, rationale, plea, and prayer. Like James Baldwin, I believe that "[n]ot everything that is faced can be changed. But nothing can be changed until it is faced" (Baldwin, 1962). Let us face the reality of our situation regarding teaching social studies content to our children. Let us face it and fix it before it is too late.

CHAPTER 1

WHERE WE ARE NOW

A Short History

From the first days of the republic, instruction in history, geography, and civics was vital to education efforts in the United States. In 1820, Thomas Jefferson wrote, "I know of no safe depository of the ultimate powers of the society but with the people themselves; and if we think them not enlightened enough to exercise their control with a wholesome discretion, the remedy is not to take power from them, but to inform their discretion through instruction" (qtd. in Carroll, 1997, p. 80). We know that the social realities of our nation's early years did not mirror the idealized goals of democracy and equality voiced in our founding documents. The pernicious institution of race-based enslavement as well as gender-, culture-, and religion-based inequities were horrific realities at the time of our nation's founding. However, the goal of a nation "E pluribus unum" was clearly stated, if not actualized, from our nation's beginning.

In the earliest days of compulsory education, social studies instruction was at the center of the curriculum. Even if not called "social studies," the curricular goals of schooling in the 18th and 19th centuries included the study of history, geography, and civics. Influential educators viewed the common school as central to promoting social harmony and ensuring that the republic would be guided by an intelligent, moral citizenry. Horace Mann, the 19th-century politician also known as the "Father of the

Common School Movement," believed that the creation of free, public, nonsectarian (although based on Protestant Christian philosophy and texts) schools throughout the growing Republic would be the "best means of achieving the moral and socioeconomic uplift of all Americans" (Warder, 2015). Social studies as a discrete content area has always borne special responsibility for inculcating the population with moral values and readying students to assume adult roles in our democratic republic (Beal & Martorella, 1994; Lybarger, 1983; Parker & Beck, 2017).

At the turn of the 21st century, however, it became an Achilles' heel of the curriculum, particularly in elementary schools, where it is relegated to "second string" after reading, English language arts, math, and science. Much research has been published examining the steady and consistent reduction in social studies instruction since 2000, especially in elementary schools (Heafner & Fitchett, 2012; Heafner et al., 2007; VanFossen, 2005; McMurren, 2007; VanFossen, 2005). Forty-four percent of districts nationally have reduced time in their elementary teaching schedules for social studies since the federal No Child Left Behind initiative began in 2002 (Fitchett et al., 2014). For those of us who lived through them, the educational and assessment reforms and legislative efforts that resulted in a reduction in social studies instruction are far too familiar: federally funded programs including No Child Left Behind and Race to the Top as well as the constant drumbeat of expectation about increasing scores on standardized tests in reading and math. Each of these has played a role, intentional or not, in the marginalization of social studies mostly felt at the elementary school level. As a graduate student participating in school observations in the late 1990s, I remember visiting an elementary school in an under-served neighborhood of Boston. As I walked through a hallway, I heard the principal telling a second-grade team meeting, "Don't let me catch any of you teaching social studies until I see these reading scores come up!" When I was a social studies methodology instructor years later, many students' stories of their work as elementary teachers in classrooms throughout New York City echoed similar themes.

State of Play Today

The issue of access to social studies teaching and learning at the elementary grades in the United States today, then, is two-fold: (1) in many places there is little to no social studies being taught at the elementary level; (2) when social studies is taught, it is often a perfunctory coverage of events or reduced to celebrations of heroes and holidays. How has this happened? High-stakes testing, standardized assessments, and local standards documents often have had as a side effect the minimization of the importance of social studies or caused it to be left out of the elementary school curriculum completely.

All elementary classroom teachers in the nation know that their primary responsibility is to teach children literacy and numeracy. This message is underscored boldly by principals, parents, and school board members in every district in every school. When this message is supported by the administration of high-stakes tests that focus exclusively on reading and math skills, most classroom teachers find little reason or support for taking time out of an already over-scheduled elementary school day to teach social studies, science, or any content that won't appear on an assessment. Consistent challenges in the United States of inadequate teacher pay, under-resourced classrooms, and unrealistic parental expectations also have a powerful impact on teachers' choices. New challenges include the realities of the COVID-19 pandemic and the multiple and profound effects it is having on teaching and learning (US Department of Education, 2021). Most recently, a coordinated political effort in more than half of US states has also had an impact. In 36 state legislatures, bills or other actions have been taken to restrict how teachers discuss issues including race, racism, sexism, gender, and human sexuality. Florida's "Parental Rights in Education" bill "prohibits classroom instruction or discussion about sexual orientation and gender identity" in elementary schools (Goldstein, 2022). To date, 14 states have passed legislation limiting the teaching of these topics (Pendharker, 2022), but "at least 36 states have adopted or introduced laws or policies that restrict teaching about race and racism" (Stout & Wilburn, 2022). A parallel effort has focused on banning books in schools around these same topics (Gabbatt, 2022). The impact on teaching around the nation goes further, however, as research shows that in 894 school districts across the nation, representing 35 percent of our student population, administrators, parents, teachers, and school board members have been affected by these efforts (Pollack et al., 2022). Under the dishonest guise of protecting K–12 students from inappropriate or unpatriotic education efforts, including a theory on systemic racism called "critical race theory," a well-funded and highly organized political minority has successfully limited the teaching of social studies in public schools. This is an organized and highly political effort to manufacture a crisis. Critical race theory is not taught in K–12 schools and does not appear in any standards or curriculum. The real goals include the disruption of discussions about racism, African enslavement, sexism, white privilege, sexual orientation, and the role of racist policies in US history (Gabriel & Goldstein, 2021;

Kingkade, 2021; Pollack et al. 2022).

Another reason that US social studies is dissolving is the fact that for much of the 20th and into the 21st centuries, scholars in the field have disagreed or voiced contentious arguments in the literature about exactly what social studies should look like in our schools (Evans, 2006). Unlike other content areas, there has been little agreement among scholars about the basics of what we should be teaching in this area. Traditionally, and still prevalent in most parts of the United States, one finds some version of the "widening horizons" or "expanding environment" social curriculum in grades K–6 that is often described as follows:

Grade K:	Me
Grade 1:	Family
Grade 2:	Neighborhood
Grade 3:	Community
Grade 4:	State or Region
Grade 5:	Nation
Grade 6:	World (Maxim, 1999, p. 21)

This curriculum has a rich and storied history in US education, going back to leading US philosopher and education scholar John Dewey's (1902) belief in the need to place the child at the center of the educational process. Historians and other scholars have argued that this curricular tradition is weak and outdated. Many have written about the need for more history or geography starting at the earliest grades to replace an otherwise boring and redundant elementary social studies curriculum about family, neighborhoods, and community helpers (Brophy &

Alleman, 2006; Hirsch, 1987; Krahenbuhl, 2019; Ravitch, 1998; Wade, 2002).

In addition, the proliferation of standards documents in the social sciences add to the complexity of effective curricular actualization. While curricular debates in reading and math focus mainly on *pedagogy* (whole language, phonics, science of reading, arithmetic, constructivist math, etc.), only social studies has major academic and research lobbies fighting over the *content* that should be taught to students (Evans, 2006; Schwartz, 2021). Note, for example, that national standards documents (many in multivolume works) exist in world history, US history, geography, economics, civics, and social studies (Center for Civic Education, 1994; Council for Economic Education, 2010; National Center for History in the Schools, 1994, 1996; National Council for Geographic Education, 2012; National Council for the Social Studies, 2010). This is, let's remember, in addition to 50 publications of state standards in social studies. How can we expect elementary-level curriculum developers, administrators, and classroom teachers to deal with all these documents and the expectations they assume? Elements of these academic arguments and some understandings of standards have filtered down to the district, school, and classroom levels. In some cases, they have helped classroom teachers and local curriculum developers define a scope and sequence for instruction, but more often they have caused confusion at the local level. This helps expand the vacuum in social studies instruction that has been filled by the expectations (and the tests that follow them) in reading and math.

Changes Afoot

There are, however, changes afoot in the United States concerning the teaching of reading (Knowledge Matters Campaign, 2021; Pondiscio, 2014). A renewed focus on the importance of content knowledge and a demand for disciplinary literacy spurred by the Common Core State Standards for English Language Arts and Literacy have helped build challenging arguments against the exclusion of content (especially social studies and science) from our elementary schools. While the transformative curricular goals of the Common Core standards in reading and math may not have been realized and their use in many schools has been challenged, the standards in reading have had an influence on state standards documents, pedagogy, and curricular choices throughout the nation (Barnum, 2019; Loveless, 2021). A major difference in the demands of the Common Core State Standards for English Language Arts and Literacy was for a greater emphasis on working with informational text and writing in the content areas (National Governors Association Center for Best Practices, 2010). "Grades 6–12 Literacy in History/Social Studies, Science, & Technical Subjects" have a clear and focused call for disciplinary literacy that is hardly being met by the dissolution of social studies in the elementary classroom. Disciplinary literacy is "the unique way that specific disciplines create, communicate and evaluate information" (Shanahan & Shanahan, 2012) and demands that students are given practice with and specifically taught how to read historical, scientific, and mathematical content.

Educators and authors such as E. D. Hirsch (1987) have been arguing for a more rigorous and content-focused curriculum in our elementary schools since the 1980s. Work by journalist Natalie Wexler (2019) and cognitive scientist David Willingham (2009) and others have thrown new light on the power of teachers to increase comprehension, vocabulary, and reading capacity by focusing on content as knowledge-building background and context for their students. This work supports research done by Merton (1968) in science and then by Walberg and Tsai (1983) on student achievement and content instruction. These researchers referred to a concept called the "Matthew effect," named after a passage from the Gospel of Matthew: "For whoever has will be given more, and they will have an abundance" (Matthew 25:29). It argues that those students exposed to more information, language, content, and knowledge earlier will both learn more and be able to show more academic success as they are better able to connect more knowledge to earlier received knowledge. Wexler shares the oft-used and commonly understood image of hook-and-loop fasteners to help describe this process. Recent scholars have continued to present data supporting the Matthew effect and its impact on student reading achievement (Cunningham & Chen, 2014). Wexler (2019) describes it in the following way: "When young children are introduced to history and science in concrete and understandable ways, chances are they'll be far better equipped to reengage with those topics with more nuance later on. At the same time, teaching disconnected comprehension skills boosts neither comprehension nor reading scores. It's just empty calories. In effect, kids are clamoring for broccoli and spinach while adults insist on a steady diet of donuts." The Thomas B. Fordham Institute published a study titled "Social Studies Instruction and Reading Comprehension: Evidence from the Early Childhood Longitudinal Study" arguing that teaching more social studies content played a role in increasing students' reading performance (Tyner & Kabourek, 2020). A growing chorus of educators and scholars from a wide variety of backgrounds is challenging the status quo of an over reliance on skill and strategy work in the reading classroom and bemoaning the lack of content-rich curriculum firmly rooted in the content areas of science and social studies (Knowledge Matters Campaign, 2021; Schmoker, 2020).

Local Realities

As we know, the lack of a national social studies curriculum in the United States makes the choice of what is taught in social studies classrooms a local decision (Schwartz, 2021). There have been arguments about this for years, and the United States remains alone on the international stage for not having shared national social studies curricula. My goal here is not to argue one position or the other or to provide a solution to this lack of a national social studies curriculum. The fact remains that state and local standards are what teachers throughout the United States use to define their curricular choices if and when they teach social studies. This system is, by definition, susceptible to local political conflicts over curriculum choices and materials selection, but the concept of local control over education is a longstanding and accepted tradition in the United States (Uerling & O'Reilly, 1989). In a fascinating 2020 comparison of high school social studies textbooks, written by the same publishers, for California and Texas, Dana Goldstein of the *New York Times* found numerous differences in content due to the unique demands of the states' standards documents. "Whole paragraphs on redlining and restrictive deeds appear only in the California editions of textbooks, partly as a result of different state standards. Texas' social studies guidelines do not mention housing discrimination at all" (Goldstein, 2020).

A cursory examination of different state standards documents wields many differences in content even while the topics that are covered might be the same. For example, in Michigan, fifth graders study early US history in a course titled Integrated United States History to 1800. In Alabama, fifth graders also study early US history in a course titled United States Studies: Beginnings to the Industrial Revolution.

In the Michigan social studies standards, content about life in West Africa (including culture, religious beliefs, customs, etc.) prior to the emergence of the European slave trade that brought millions of enslaved Africans to the North American colonies is included. Teachers are also expected to help students understand the ways of life of both enslaved and free Africans who lived in colonial America:

MICHIGAN Social Studies Standards Grade 5
U1.3 African Life Before the 16th Century
Describe the lives of peoples living in West Africa prior to the 16th century. 5 – U1.3.1 Use maps to locate the major regions of Africa (North Africa, West Africa, Central Africa, East Africa, Southern Africa). 5 – U1.3.2 Describe the life and cultural development of people living in West Africa before the 16th century with respect to economic (the ways people made a living) and family structures, and the growth of states, towns, and trade.

Analyze the development of the slave system in the Americas and its impact. 5 – U2.2.1 Describe Triangular Trade, including: • the trade routes. • the people and goods that were traded. • the Middle Passage. • the impact on life in Africa. 5 – U2.2.2 Describe the lives of enslaved Africans and free Africans, including fugitive and escaped slaves in the American colonies. 5 – U2.2.3 Describe how enslaved and free Africans struggled to retain elements of their diverse African histories and cultures to develop distinct African-American identities. (Michigan Department of Education, 2019, pp. 44, 46)

In Alabama's fifth-grade social studies standards, however,

there is no mention of this content and no expectation for teaching or learning about the history or culture of any of the people involved in the brutal enslavement of millions of Africans. The topic itself is treated in the language of the Alabama standards solely as an economic system of labor, as if it existed outside any cultural or other context (except to note that slave labor was brought to the Americas by a "Northern colonial shipping industry"):

> ALABAMA Social Studies Standards Grade 5
> 6) Describe colonial economic life and labor systems in the Americas.
> - Recognizing centers of slave trade in the Western Hemisphere and the establishment of the Triangular Trade Route
>
> **Evidence Of Student Attainment:**
> Students:
> - Describe colonial economic life and labor systems in the Americas.
> - Describe centers of slave trade in the Western Hemisphere and the establishment of the Triangular Trade Route. ...
>
> **Knowledge:**
> Students know:
> - Each colony's economic life and labor system was unique and based on the geographic location of the colony.
> - Most slaves came from a variety of countries in Africa and were brought to the Americas by slave traders using the Triangular Trade Route.
>
> **Skills:**
> Students are able to:

- Locate each colony on a physical and political map.
- Describe and explain the types of labor used in each colony (indentured servitude, slaves, free blacks, merchants, farmers, shipping, fishing/whaling, among others).
- Trace, examine and evaluate the Triangular Trade Route and its impact on colonial economy and labor systems.

Understanding:

Students understand that:

- Different labor systems were used to build and grow each of the 13 colonies.
- Slave labor was brought to the Americas by the Northern colonial shipping industry and purchased and used in the Caribbean islands and Southern colonies. (Alabama Learning Exchange, 2017)

The current legislative efforts in a majority of US states to limit, suppress, or radically diminish teaching about specific historical topics such as racism are deeply troubling. Some bills and laws are particularly vague such as in Georgia, where the state board adopted a resolution that does not allow lessons that "promote one race over the other." Texas has adopted limits on how teachers can discuss racism and sexism (Hicks, 2021). Other states such as Tennessee have adopted policies whereby teachers can lose their jobs for running afoul of the new laws or board decisions (Stout & LeMee, 2021).

Yale University professor and scholar of totalitarianism Timothy Snyder (2021) equates efforts that hope to limit teaching about enslavement of people of African heritage; race-based legal strategies such as voter suppression, segregation, and red-lining; and the question of whether racism has been codified in our current legal and social systems to the "memory laws" instituted in Russia in the early 2000s. In his powerful argument, Snyder describes many of the restrictive rules currently in place in Russian schools regarding teaching or discussing historical events in Ukraine and elsewhere during World War II. Snyder argues

C3 Framework Organization

	Dimention 2: Applying Disciplinary Tools and Concepts	Dimention 3: Evaluating Sources and Using Evidence	Dimention 4: Communicating Conclusions and Taking Informed Action
Developing Questions and Planning Inquiries	Civics	Gathering and Evaluating Sources	Communicating and Critiquing Conclusions
	Economics		
	Geography	Developing Claims and Using Evidence	Taking Informed Action
	History		

Dimention I: Developing Questions and Planning Inquiries

From NCSS website: https://www.socialstudies.org/standards/c3

that the current laws in some US states have similar goals as they place restrictions on teaching certain historical realities and privilege student "feelings" over the actual building of historical analysis skills in students (Snyder, 2021). While it may be too soon to make any historical analyses about this recent phenomenon, I do believe that history will look back on these efforts as one piece in a complex political and social drama currently playing out in our society.

C3 & IDM: Potential Paths Forward

Two important works in the field of social studies education have been published in the last 10 years that are helpful to our efforts to better understand how social studies needs to be understood in the 21st century. In 2013 the National Council for the Social Studies published a framework titled "College, Career, and Civic Life (C3) Framework for Social Studies State Standards: Guidance for Enhancing the Rigor of K–12 Civics, Economics, Geography, and History," a document that is commonly known as "the C3." The framework does an excellent job of presenting to teachers, administrators, and parents ways that local and state standards can be used to incorporate high-quality social studies education in every community. The framework presents four dimensions that should be kept in focus when social studies teaching and learning happen in schools:

1. Developing questions and planning inquiries;
2. Applying disciplinary concepts and tools;
3. Evaluating sources and using evidence; and
4. Communicating conclusions and taking informed action. (p. 12)

The C3 framework hoped to help remedy and respond to the need for an increase in K–12 social studies education and promote a higher level of integration, especially at the elementary levels, with English language arts instruction and the development of disciplinary literacy skills as demanded by the Common Core ELA standards.

The focus of the C3 framework is inquiry-based instruction. A recent publication from authors Kathy Swan, John Lee, and S. G. Grant is Inquiry Design Model: Building Inquiries in Social Studies. This text provides an excellent model for teaching social studies while incorporating and supporting the concept of inquiry-based instruction. This work followed an important and impressive effort made in concert with hundreds of teachers as they created inquiry-based curricular models for New York State following the recommendations of the C3. These model units, which can be found at https://www.engageny.org/resource/new-york-state-k-12-social-studies-resource-toolkit, are great examples of bridging the ideals of inquiry design and practical classroom applications. The work allowed Swan and colleagues to focus their ideas on inquiry teaching and learning with actual curriculum design to help teachers see how these ideas could be put into practice. As the authors state:

> Over the course of a year, with the help of committed and innovate group of K–12 teachers, we kicked the tires of IDM [Inquiry Design Model] trying to hone a way to do curriculum that would elevate and further articulate inquiry but not annoy teachers with over-prescriptions and other lesson plan tedium. And, we did our fair share of kicking. (Swan et al., 2018, p. 5)

I believe that these two texts about the C3 and the IDM should be read and discussed by every social studies chair, principal, faculty, and curriculum design team. There are three concepts found in both the C3 document and the IDM text that I feel are worth the effort to focus on specifically here: content, sources, and evidence-based arguments. I would also like to present some ideas about how these concepts might look within the parameters of an eighth-grade social studies unit.

Content

As mentioned earlier, content, while defined by local and state standards documents, can be troubling because there is always "too much to teach." This has been a perennial problem for teachers, textbook authors, and curriculum designers. Inquiry can help teachers focus on particularly important questions that assist students in truly engaging with content while making connections to their lives and current realities. Swan et al. (2018) talk about finding a "content angle" to help teachers negotiate the issue of trying to cover all of the content for which they are responsible. They describe this as a creative process for teachers to use their professional capacity that also demands a true understanding of the standards and content issues. "In the inquiry design process, teachers are crafting a way for students to become more fluent with content. Standards are a starting point, but teachers are the mediators of a process that makes standards and content accessible. It is here that teachers have to find a content angle to bring the inquiry design process to life" (p. 22).

A focus on specific inquiry topics aids teachers and students in deepening their understanding of content topics and can also help both groups engage with content in new and more sustainable ways (Barton & Levstick, 2004; Hmelo et al., 2000; Kuhlthau et al., 2007; Shepherd, 1998). This becomes even more challenging in some places, however, as I have noted due to recent legislative efforts in many states that restrict the teaching of important components and content about US history. Most state social studies standards at Grade 8 include the historic period of social upheaval in the 1960s in the United States. Part of this study is often about the protest movements of the period, those against and in support of the war in Vietnam, protests for equal rights for women, student rights, and the Civil Rights MC3 website of teacher resources (http://c3teachers.

org/inquiries/patriotism) and can provide an example of the way that interesting, standards-based content, sourcing, and evidence-based arguments can be used in practice to build student knowledge and skills.

Sources

Helping students access and understand various sources has always been an important goal of social studies education. With the emergence of the digital world and the constant onslaught of millions of pieces of information, misinformation, and disinformation in our pockets, the capacity for students to truly understand sources is vital. Social studies teaching and learning provide a unique capacity for students to engage with and more deeply understand the role sources play in building knowledge. Working with sources is a key component of the inquiry design model and of using inquiry to teach social studies at the K–12 levels. Swan et al. (2018) devote a chapter in their book to describing the use of "source logic" in the inquiry process. They believe that "good sources bring inquiry to life" (p. 78), and working with sources should be a mainstay of every social studies teacher's unit and lesson planning. Scholars and education groups have been helping teachers better understand how to work with sources for years. One of the most important is the Stanford History Education Group (SHEG) at Stanford University. The educators at SHEG support teachers to "investigate historical questions by employing reading strategies such as sourcing, contextualizing, corroborating, and close reading. … Students evaluate the trustworthiness of multiple perspectives on historical issues and learn to make historical claims backed by documentary evidence" (https:// sheg.stanford.edu/history-lessons). One of the strategies mentioned in the SHEG document, contextualization, can be an especially big challenge for many teachers. Contextualization generally means placing a source in its proper perspective, but this is not an easy task. Students need a certain amount of background knowledge and support to help them understand the time and place, author intent, and other economic, social, and political contexts that might surround any source they encounter. Practice with this skill is fundamental in building student capacity for deep historical understandings (Huijgen et al., 2018; Wineburg, 1991; Woyshner, 2010). It is also necessary for anyone who watches television or surfs the Internet! The sources we are exposed to—YouTube videos, political speeches, news reports, or research articles—demand contextualization for us to understand them. In an age of "fake news," growing AI capacities, and "deep fakes," this need becomes greater, albeit more complex.

Founding member of SHEG and leading education scholar Sam Wineburg has stated that this ability of students to work with, understand, verify, compare, and differentiate sources becomes even more critical in our digital age. "On every question we face as citizens—to raise the minimum wage, to legalize marijuana, to tax sugary drinks, to abolish private prisons, you name it—sham sources jostle for our attention right next to trustworthy ones. Failing to teach kids the difference is educational negligence" (qtd. in Hess, 2021).

While working through the "Is Protest Patriotic?" inquiry, for example, students are challenged to examine sources from a variety of points of view about the concept of protest in a democratic society. These sources are from the period under study (news accounts, speeches, video interviews) as well as important historical documents that address the issue, in this case excerpts from Thomas Paine's series of articles from *The American Crisis* (1776–1783). They see and read the actions and words of protesters against the war in Vietnam, for example, while also reading arguments in support of President Nixon's Indochina war strategy as a way of fighting the spread of communism. During a rich, inquiry-based learning experience, students can make connections to their own experiences, which helps them connect to the material. Only with exposure to multiple examples and a variety of types of sources can students deepen their understandings of the complex nature of historical periods. As historian and educational scholar Christine Woyshner (2010) states, "Too often historical inquiry stops short at teaching students to interpret primary sources devoid of context and without a repeating cycle that includes connecting their lives to the topic, wondering about it and its importance, and reflecting on what was learned and its significance" (p. 42).

Evidence-Based Arguments

Helping students make and defend arguments on positions, opinions, or ideas is another key goal of social studies education. Using the inquiry method helps give students the practice they need to find the necessary source material and use those materials to make strong, evidence-based arguments. While this is a goal of social studies education, it is also a skill demanded at all grades in the Common Core State Standards for English Language Arts and Literacy and in many state English language arts standards, even as early as Grade 1. Students are expected to "Write arguments to support claims in an analysis of substantive topics or texts using valid reasoning and relevant and sufficient evidence" (CCSS ELA Anchor

Standards for Writing, Grade 1; http://www.corestandards. org/ELA-Literacy/CCRA/W/1/). Please read that standard again. It is from CCSS ELA Grade 1. Don't you wish some adults, including those at the highest levels of power, could do that?

The capacity for individuals to write arguments and support claims with evidence is also a requirement for a functioning democracy (Hillocks, 2010; Marzano, Pickering & Pollock, 2001). Every person who needs to solve problems at home, at work, in their community, and at the national level should be willing, ready, and able to do this. "Tied to a content rich curriculum, focusing on argument and its corollaries have unparalleled power to make school interesting—and to prepare students for college, careers, citizenship or any achievement test that will ever come their way" (Schmoker & Graff, 2011).

In our media-saturated world, students see and hear individuals who are given a platform to make arguments and proclamations that are evidence-free or based on inconclusive or simply false data. Many of these people go unchallenged when they make these arguments. More frequently, the arguments are amplified by deceitful individuals, profit-hungry media organizations, and social media algorithms. A recent example is the collection of fabricated stories regarding irregularities and cheating in numerous states during the 2020 US presidential election, collectively known as the "big lie." Unscrupulous attorneys, politicians, media personalities, journalists, and civil servants promulgated a series of conspiracy theories and false claims challenging the validity of the election outcomes because their preferred candidate did not win. These theories and claims were then amplified by online and television media organizations such as One America Network, Newsmax, and, most especially, Fox News (Long,

2021). These lies and fabrications were used as rationale by certain groups and individuals to attack the US Capitol building on January 6, 2021, to try to stop the election certification process (Smith, 2022). These false claims continue to hold sway over many US citizens, even after high-profile promoters, such as attorney Sidney Powell, admit they were lies. When defending Powell against defamation charges in court, Powell's lawyers stated, "No reasonable person would conclude that the statements [she made about election irregularities] were truly statements of fact" (qtd. in McCarthy, 2021).

Our students see, hear, and read these evidence-free, bogus arguments, as do their parents, neighbors, and grandparents. Sometimes teachers are even taken in by false, unverified arguments. We must work to help students understand that only evidence-based arguments should be acceptable in the arena of civic, educated, and professional discourse. And they must learn that the evidence they use to support their arguments in and outside of class are relevant, research based, and factual and come from reputable sources.

Swan et al. (2018) state that "if students do not have the opportunity to express their arguments in powerful ways, we have essentially taken the social out of social studies" (p. 105). Their work on creating inquiries builds to a final phase whereby students have multiple opportunities to express evidence-based arguments for the compelling questions under study. They state, "We created the inquiry design model (IDM) to enable social studies students to wrestle with important questions of the past and present and to advance our society by answering those questions with arguments backed by evidence" (p. 140).

This work is neither easy nor fast. It takes time, effort, consistency, alignment, and review. This consistent and patient effort, however, also builds the power of integrating inquiry practice throughout all grade levels. Each year presents new projects and possibilities for students to flex their growing inquiry and critical-thinking muscles with more complex historic, geographic, economic, and civic content.

In our Grade 8 example from the EngageNY website, we see students presenting evidence-based arguments on a challenging, multifaceted issue. After a deep dive into the questions and sources presented in the unit, students are challenged to "Construct an argument (e.g., detailed outline, poster, essay) that addresses the compelling question (Is protest patriotic?) using specific claims and relevant evidence from historical sources while acknowledging competing views" (http://c3teachers.org/inquiries/patriotism/).

Social studies scholar Walter Parker writes about the inquiry design process:

> What the inquiry design model aims to do is educate the inherent human capacity for inquiry, shaping it from its everyday, casual form to its more rigorous, scientific form— from undisciplined to disciplined inquiry. This is why children and youth are sent to school. This is what social studies education is for. It furnishes students' minds with the subject matter of history and the social sciences and it empowers them to reason with evidence— sourcing, contextualizing, corroborating, questioning. This liberates them to think outside the boxes of their upbringing and the status quo. Inquiry is a blade that can cut thought the crust of conventional wisdom, leading the thinker into the unknown, thinking

the not-yet-thought. This is its social justice rationale. All of our students should have access to it. (qtd. in Swan et al., 2018, p. 4)

Meeting the Challenges

We have seen in this "Where We Are Now" section that while there are grave challenges regarding the teaching of social studies in our nation today, there also exist amazing researchers, writers, and teachers who are doing high-quality work in the field. Solid curricula, sound pedagogy, and committed practitioners exist and are changing lives throughout the country. We need to support and replicate all the good work being done so that more students are intellectually challenged and more high-quality social studies instruction happens every year.

CHAPTER 2

WHERE WE NEED TO BE

21st Century Skills

As the first quarter of the 21st century ends, our society is facing daunting challenges. I believe that supporting more inquiry-based, high-quality social studies instruction is a critically important way that educators can play an important role in dealing with these challenges.

Since the 1990s, educators have been concerned by what the 21st century would demand of students. In the first quarter of the century, "21st-century skills" is a phrase that has become quite common among educators to outline four skills that are said to be most useful for student success now and in our immediate future. These skills, found in the "Frameworks for 21st Century Learning," published by the nonprofit educational organizations Partnership for 21st Century Skills (P21) and Battelle for Kids, are critical thinking, communication, collaboration, and creativity (Partnership for 21st Century Learning, 2002). I'd like to look at each of these to illustrate how a sound social studies education can support student growth in each area.

Critical Thinking

While there are many definitions of critical thinking, Elder and Paul (2008) explain it as "that mode of thinking—about any subject, content or problem—in which the thinker improves the quality of his or her thinking by skillfully taking charge of the structures inherent in thinking and imposing intellectual standards upon them"

(Foundation for Critical Thinking, 2019). Critical thinking is not a new concept. Educators have argued for generations (Beyer, 1988; Bloom, 1956; Dewey, 1916; Ennis, 1962; Halpern, 1998) about the nuances of the term and the need to improve critical thinking and critical-thinking education for our youth. In 1906, William G. Sumner described education in critical thinking as producing those who are "slow to believe. They can hold things as possible or probable in all degrees, without certainty or without pain. They can wait for evidence and weigh evidence. They can resist appeals to their dearest principles. Education in the critical faculty is the only education of which it can be truly said that it makes good citizens" (pp. 632–633).

However, the changes wrought by the advent of new technologies and ever-changing structures of society and economies demand a renewed focus on critical thinking for success in the 21st century. The complexity of these new problems and the challenges that we currently face demand a population more capable of moving beyond simple recall, comprehension, and application to advanced and critical stages of thinking, defined by Bloom (1956) as analysis, synthesis, evaluation, and creation. In my 40 years of classroom teaching and professional development work with teachers, building critical-thinking skills was always about helping teachers and students learn how to ask questions, first by creating a classroom environment where questioning was affirmed and supported, and second by guiding students to build capacity in solid questioning so that they understood the power of well-crafted and focused questions to try to better understand problems and issues under study. Social studies content provides opportunities for this at all grade levels. Challenging kindergarten students with the question of why they should be responsible, asking third graders to explain how sharing and trading across cultures and countries can affect their lives, demanding that eighth graders answer the question "Is Greed Good?" while studying the Gilded Age, or challenging eleventh graders with the task of understanding if nonviolent protests were successful during the 1960s Civil Rights Movement are examples of the types of lessons that bolster students' critical-thinking capacities by building content-driven and question-driven instruction (Foundation for Critical Thinking, 2022). When we deny access to these lessons and the questions and dilemmas they pose, we are withholding from students the chance to better develop the critical-thinking capacities they will need in the future.

Communication

The ability to communicate clearly and effectively is a basic function of education, no matter the content area. However, when we think about communication as a successful life and professional skill in the future, we must also remember that it involves more than simply speaking and writing clearly. This is where social studies content can make a difference. Social studies curricula can provide students with multiple opportunities for exposition about and actual practice in the role that effective communication strategies can play in our lives. Historical examples abound where students can learn about how effective communication affected our history, including dialogue and negotiations between political leaders as well as everyday people across time. Examples to study include James Madison's fascinating Federalist Papers and Anne Frank's beautiful, heartfelt diary entries. In these and so many other historical documents and sources, individuals and groups used their communication skills to share important ideas and have unquestionably changed the world.

To help understand how communication efforts can be denied or used to suppress historical remembering, students can study how Mary E. Jones Parrish (1923/2009) chronicled the horrible violence in Tulsa, Oklahoma, in 1921. Parrish's African American neighborhood of Greenwood—known as "Black Wall Street"—including her successful business school was burned and ravaged by a white mob in May 1921. This book became evidence of a historical reality that was dismissed and rebranded by a culpable local government (Lackmeyer, 2021).

There are many examples of speeches used as important communication vehicles to promote important causes and ideas such as Dr. Martin Luther King Jr.'s powerful "I Have a Dream" speech in 1963. Other examples include Representative Barbara Jordan's compelling 1974 statement on the power and purpose of the Constitution during the Nixon impeachment hearings. President Ronald Reagan, quoting the Puritan leader John Winthrop, used the "shining city upon a hill" image to make his view of the United States come alive during his farewell address in 1989; after the September 11, 2001, attacks on New York and Washington, DC, President George W. Bush spoke of how the attacks "shattered steel but they cannot dent the steel of American resolve." These and many others give students examples of how communication can be used for social, cultural, and political purposes. In 2021, the National History Day theme of study was "Communication in History: The Key to Understanding," which promulgated a plethora of primary and secondary source resources on communication from organizations such as the National Archives, Library of Congress, and the National Endowment of the Humanities (National History Day, 2022).

Collaboration

According to the P21 framework, those who can truly communicate in the future will also need to be able to collaborate with others, be flexible and make compromises, and work effectively in teams made up of diverse members (Partnership for 21st Century Learning, 2002). This capacity for collaboration does not come naturally to everyone, and like most important skills it must be explicitly taught to students. Putting students' desks into sets of three or four does not create collaborative teams. Helping students see the steps necessary for a successful collaborative project and giving them ample opportunities to practice are key.

Almost all inquiry-based social studies activities are built on the premise of collaborative work. Offering these lessons to students on a regular basis is one way to guarantee that they receive the practice they need to learn collaborative skills. Modeling collaboration is also an excellent way to help students learn. Many social studies teachers work with ELA, dramatic arts, and other colleagues to plan and implement lessons and units. These are excellent, real-life examples for students about the power of collaboration for success. Social studies content is also full of stories of collaboration. These stories make for real-life examples of how collaboration—on a political, economic, or personal level—has affected the history of our nation and our world. Examples abound in our social studies curricula, such as the Wright brothers and the birth of air travel or the incredible collaboration between Alice Paul, Emmiline Pankhurst, and other women to highlight the injustices regarding voting rights for women more than a century ago. Collaboration played a key role among different individuals, groups, and ethnicities in various labor and human rights struggles since our nation's founding.

The stories of collaboration, and the individuals, groups, and activities surrounding them, have great power. New brain research is showing us examples of how stories can connect us and help build understanding and comprehension as well as heighten our perspective-taking abilities (Renken, 2020).

Creativity

While not exclusive to social studies content, creative individuals, ideas, and behaviors make up a big part of the story of our past. Creative, talented individuals from Leonardo to Du Bois have helped shape our past and present and are worthy of our study. Helping students understand the power of creativity and how creative individuals in our past have shaped our present is one of the main purposes of social studies education. An example of creativity and its impact can be found by studying the life of the mid-20th-century Hollywood actress Hedy Lamarr. Few realize that while a beautiful and talented actress, Lamarr also had an inquisitive, creative mind that was constantly working to solve complex problems she observed around her. At the start of World War II, she and a colleague created a radio frequency system that they offered to the US Navy to help secure wartime communications. While the Navy did not use the idea then, it later served as the basis for our current GPS and Bluetooth technology systems, earning Lamarr the title "mother of wi-fi" (Cheslak, 2018). A lesson plan on this fascinating, creative individual from the National Women's History Museum can be found online (https://www.womenshistory.org/resources/lesson-plan/hedy-lamarr).

Like the other 21st-century skills mentioned above, creativity is not something that a student can memorize or regurgitate on a test. The development of one's creative skills set is a lifelong process. Traditionally, schools have been a place where creativity has sometimes been allowed to flourish but was often sacrificed for order, consistency, and quiet. In our understanding of education today, we must work to develop the creative spaces where students can feel intellectually challenged. These two concepts, intellectualism and creativity, should not be opposing concepts but must link together in our schools so that students will be ready for the world that awaits them. "Creativity," says Lindsay Patterson (2018), "allows an entrepreneur to disconnect from the accustomed and move into uncharted territories with an aim to discern unique and useful solutions. It has, therefore, become essential for both leaders and employees to develop creative skills." Learning through an inquiry-based social studies lesson allows students to develop a wide range of creative skills. Most importantly, it affords them the opportunity to think creatively, probe for new solutions to difficult problems, and wonder about the exciting and magnificent world around them that they have yet to discover (Donovan et al., 2014; Kupers et al., 2018; Rotherham & Willingham, 2010).

CHAPTER 3

WHY IT MATTERS:
THREE ARGUMENTS FOR MORE SOCIAL STUDIES INSTRUCTION

Common Good

In recent years, scholars and social commentators have warned that the fabric of our society is tearing more (Edsall, 2021; Putnam, 2000). Fewer individuals seem to understand or appreciate our responsibility to others and to how every citizen has a role to play in making our communities, cities, states, nation, and world a better place. Concern about this fracturing of society drives my first argument for an increase in inquiry-based social studies education. Identity politics, narrow self-definitions, and one-issue voting have eroded a sense of shared identity for many Americans. In short, many of us have forgotten about or were never taught to truly understand the concept of the common good.

Social studies plays a huge role in helping students learn to appreciate the benefits of working toward a greater common good. From understanding the challenges of history and geography to exploring the ways economics works for or against us as members of the community and as individuals, social studies helps students develop an appreciation, at a deep level, for how our actions and choices affect not only us, not only our families and friends, but everyone with whom we share the planet. In Bowling Alone, Putnam (2000) theorizes that the loss of "social capital" or that connection from membership in community-based affinity groups, religious congregations, and neighborhood organizations plays an important role in Americans' seeming lack of understanding about what it means to take part in efforts for the common good, and this has a potentially negative impact on our democratic processes. While membership in online groups has grown, membership in locally active, physically present groups has declined. Putnam argues that these two types of membership are completely different, and it's the face-to-face, person-to-person interaction with others that helps us continue to grow the bonds of friendship and relationship that make connections real.

Others have examined the growth in beliefs about conspiracy theories and demonization of political opponents in the online age. While these realities have been present since the founding of our nation, the accessibility of the internet has changed how their dynamics play out. The combination of easy access to internet information, algorithms of social media companies, and lack of alternative sources of information have caused more Americans to move into a netherworld of internet-based information that is often incorrect and dangerous. A recent study by the nonpartisan Public Religion Research Institute (2021) found that 15 percent of all Americans surveyed accepts the views of the ever-shifting, conspiracy theory QAnon that believes levers of power in US politics and economics are controlled by a cabal of Satan-worshipping child molesters. Important research carried out at Stanford University also shows how susceptible students are to online misinformation. While reviewing a site on climate science, 96 percent of surveyed high school students did not understand the site's ties to the fossil fuel industry. Sixty-six percent could not distinguish paid advertisements from news reports on a website. "Over half believed that an anonymously posted Facebook video, shot in Russia, provided 'strong evidence' of US voter fraud" (Breakstone et al., 2022).

Misinformation and disinformation live, grow, and expand on the internet. The algorithms of the social media companies and the echo-chamber nature of our viewing habits mean that we hear more of the same story, often leading us down rabbit holes that sometimes have little relation to reality or verifiable, evidence-based truth. This is the reality of the current (and probably future) world in which we live. We must equip students to survive and thrive in this world. That means a renewed focus on inquiry, analysis, and demand for evidence. As the SHEG research shows, it also means a renewed focus on media technology skills that are woven throughout the entirety of the K–12 school curriculum. Joan Donovan (2020), the research director of the Shorenstein Center on Media, Politics and Public Policy at Harvard, wrote, "Like secondhand smoke, misinformation damages the quality of public life. Every conspiracy theory, every propaganda or disinformation campaign, affects people—and the expense of not responding can grow exponentially over time." Our most recent public health crisis sadly offers more examples of the power of misinformation and the potentially deadly results. Individuals' incorrect beliefs about COVID-19 and vaccines and their refusal to accept the science behind them have cost millions of lives, imperiled the health and safety of millions more, lengthened the crisis timeline, and had devastating effects on many communities (Loomba et al., 2021).

This situation is only getting more complicated as society's technological capacities increase. While misinformation and disinformation often take textual forms, one of the more terrifying realities facing us is the arrival of the "deep fake," videos and visual forms that can present a visual representation of someone or something that is fake and created or manipulated to look real (Schwartz, 2018). In 2019, Chesney and Citron published an important paper discussing the challenges and potential threats of this new use of technology:

> Deep fakes will allow individuals to live in their own subjective realities, where beliefs can be supported by manufactured "facts." When basic empirical insights provoke heated contestation, democratic discourse has difficulty proceeding. In a marketplace of ideas flooded with deep-fake videos and audio, truthful facts will have difficulty emerging from the scrum. (p. 1178)

Helping students to better understand and differentiate between real and imagined data will be a key element in their future success. Yet, we know it is not enough. As social studies scholar Joel Westheimer (2015) challenges,

> Fighting misinformation and disinformation is a huge challenge, but even that is not enough. Democratic societies require citizens who can think and act in ethically thoughtful ways. Schools need the kinds of classroom practices that teach students to recognize ambiguity and conflict in "factual" content and to see human conditions and aspirations as complex and contested. (p. 480)

This understanding of the common good must also include a commitment to antiracist and anti-oppression education for all students. Our future as a strong and diverse nation depends on students clearly understanding the complex roles that race, power, and diversity have played in our nation's unique and fascinating history. Students must have a complete and thoughtful understanding of the role that race-based enslavement played in US history and economics; the role of immigrants in our story, yesterday and today; and how the complex, fractious, emotional, difficult but often beautiful relationships between African, Asian, European, Latino, and Native American populations have created who we are as a nation. To this end, social studies must always be presented as an antiracist discipline. From kindergarten lessons on what it means to share equally with others through high school lessons on the challenges of racism in many of our systems, all students deserve to be taught how patriotic and proudly "American" it is to work against racist, sexist, and oppressive views, actions, and systems.

Growth of AI

The issues of deep fakes and many other challenges are in part attributable to the ever-growing role of artificial intelligence (AI) in our world. My second argument for an increase in social studies education includes facing the reality of AI in our lives head-on. I am not arguing that AI is necessarily bad or that it is the harbinger of the end of civilization as we know it. I simply feel we should recognize the increasingly complex capacity of computers, robots, and other technologies in our lives and, most importantly, in students' futures. We need to recognize the reality and then challenge ourselves as educators to consider how we are dealing with that reality. The World Economic Forum (2018) has stated that "65% of children entering elementary school today will ultimately end up working in completely new job types that don't yet exist." This is a stunning admission of the fact that, as teachers, we are no longer responsible for teaching students how to do their future jobs. I'm not sure we ever were, to be honest, but some would have made the argument through the years that students must learn certain facts in school so that they may have successful lives.

I still believe that students must learn certain facts in school, but this statistic and research on the future of technologies make me believe that what is more important is for us to teach students how to process information; how to evaluate, analyze, and interpret data; and how to think critically about what is presented to them so that they are ready for the technologies ahead. The Stanford History Education Group (SHEG) study mentioned earlier is instructive for us here. It is proof of our need for a renewal of media literacy to help students navigate the world today. You can access a copy of the report online (https://stacks. stanford.edu/file/druid:cz440cm8408/Students%27%20 Civic%20Online%20Reasoning_2021.pdf).

I also believe that one of our main goals in K–12 education should be giving students the gifts and tools they need to come up with answers to questions that we do not yet know. Authors of a report by Boston Consulting Group titled "The Future of Jobs in the Era of AI" compared the impact of AI on work through 2030 across three countries: Germany, Australia, and the United States. They had this to say about the situation in the United States:

> Increased job automation will also create significant opportunities. Primarily, it will enable workers to undertake higher-value tasks. For example, the removal of

mundane, repetitive tasks in legal, accounting, administrative, and similar professions opens the possibility for employees to take on more strategic roles. This also illustrates how automation will affect not only blue-collar jobs but white-collar occupations as well. Meanwhile, core human abilities—such as empathy, imagination, creativity, and emotional intelligence, which cannot be replicated by technology—will become more valuable. The supply of talent for occupations that require these abilities—such as health care workers, teachers, and counselors—is currently limited, causing the high shortfalls we see in these job families. At the same time, crises such as the COVID-19 pandemic underscore the importance of these occupations in ensuring societal well-being. (Strack et al., 2021)

Some say that up to 16 percent of US jobs will be replaced by robots and other AI mechanisms by 2025 (LeClair & Gownder, 2016). But no matter what the future of AI may bring, we will still need responsible, educated thinkers to help us navigate this new world. In a 2018 publication from the World Economic Forum (2018) titled "Harnessing Artificial Intelligence for the Earth," the authors state,

Many emerging AI solutions could have enormous impacts on the ways we live and work, but industry-led solutions may be designed and developed by a small group of people with a limited perspective. Increasingly, there will need to be diversity in AI development and use, including significantly more interaction among technology practitioners, domain and sectoral experts and philosophers, lawyers, psychologists and others, in order to develop, deploy and champion holistic AI mechanisms and solutions. (p. 21)

Kevin Kelly (2016), the cofounder of *WIRED Magazine*, argues that the continued development of AI will challenge us to reexamine what it means to be human.

> We've been redefining what it means to be human. Over the past 60 years, as mechanical processes have replicated behaviors and talents we thought were unique to humans, we've had to change our minds about what sets us apart. As we invent more species of AI, we will be forced to surrender more of what is supposedly unique about humans. Each step of surrender—we are not the only mind that can play chess, fly a plane, make music, or invent a mathematical law—will be painful and sad. We'll spend the next three decades—indeed, perhaps the next century—in a permanent identity crisis, continually asking ourselves what humans are good for. If we aren't unique toolmakers, or artists, or moral ethicists, then what, if anything, makes us special? In the grandest irony of all, the greatest benefit of an everyday, utilitarian AI will not be increased productivity or an economics of abundance or a new way of doing science—although all those will happen. The greatest benefit of the arrival of artificial intelligence is that AIs will help define humanity. (p. 129)

Kelly's comments on the definition of humanity might border on the hyperbolic, but the research and data continue to support my basic argument that in the future, those with the capacity to be flexible, inquisitive, understand perspectives, and navigate through sources and data to make evidence-based arguments will indeed be the people who will succeed. Social studies, once again, can play a critically important role in helping prepare students for the barrage of information—both real and imagined—that will present itself to them in their lifetimes. We must begin at the earliest grades helping students understand how to read, source, and analyze the data, verbal and visual, that come before them. Working with primary and secondary sources as they progress through inquiry-based lessons and units on a wide variety of social studies standards-based topics and questions will give students the content knowledge necessary to build background and the practice in applying the evaluation, analysis, and interpretation skills they will need for the rest of their lives.

The politicization of public health requirements during the most recent global public health crisis is another good example of why this matters. Wearing masks to prevent the spread of COVID-19 should be seen as a public health responsibility. Instead, mask wearing became a symbol of the government "telling me what to do," and not wearing a mask became in some places a marker of "individual freedom"; both turned an evidence-based scientific and medical fact into a political football. The political philosopher Michael Sandel has said, "The wearing of masks has become a flash point of partisan disagreement, a new front in the culture wars. ... The resistance to wearing a mask is not about public health; it's about politics" (qtd. in Walsh, 2020).

With strong social studies education at every grade for every child, there are many opportunities for teachers to help students understand what true civic duty means and how personal independence doesn't need to be selfish. Social studies can help students understand the many ways one can be patriotic and turn our talents toward others as our ancestors did during earlier crises in our history. Examples abound of ordinary citizens making extraordinary impacts by stepping up and speaking out. In May 2020, 17-year-old Darnella Frazier filmed the murder of George Floyd by police officers on a Minneapolis street. Her footage refuted the official police report on Floyd's arrest and death (Izadi, 2021). This footage helped to ignite a summer of protest and spurred the public conversation on race relations, civil rights, and the role of the police in the United States and around the world. Following the January 6, 2021, attack on the US Capitol in Washington, DC, government officials and FBI agents have relied heavily on individual citizens adept at working with social media and video footage for help in identifying those involved in the attack. These ordinary citizens are aiding the effort to bring those who attempted to disrupt the peaceful transfer of power to justice (Reilly, 2022).

Examining community problems and working toward community-based solutions can show students how collaboration and listening make a difference and how isolation, denialism, and selfishness can cripple communities and shorten citizens' lives. Studying how earlier generations sacrificed so much for us to have what we do can build empathy and help students see how we stand on the shoulders of those people who came before us.

This understanding of the common good must also include a commitment to antiracist and anti-oppression education for all students. Our future as a strong and diverse nation depends on students clearly understanding the complex roles that race, power, and diversity have played in our nation's unique and fascinating history. Students must have a complete and thoughtful understanding of the role that race-based enslavement played in US history and economics; the role of immigrants in our story, yesterday and today; and how the complex, fractious, emotional, difficult but often beautiful relationships between African, Asian, European, Latino, and Native American populations have created who we are as a nation. To this end, social studies must always be presented as an antiracist discipline. From kindergarten lessons on what it means to share equally with others through high school lessons on the challenges of racism in many of our systems, all students deserve to be taught how patriotic and proudly "American" it is to work against racist, sexist, and oppressive views, actions, and systems.

Our Government and Our Earth

My third argument focuses on the unique role of our democratic republic in the United States and on the climate crisis: the greatest threat facing the world today. I am worried that our current lack of social studies education may cause the fabric of our system of government to tear and rip apart. Educating students in both the history of our system and in the practical applications of how our system works are key goals of K–12 social studies education (Barton & Levstik, 2004). If we do not take the time, focus, or energy to do this, we risk losing a generation or more who don't understand the complicated legacy of our nation's founding or the immense possibility of our system's future.

Two recent works shine a light on the fragility of democracy as a system of government in the United States and around the world. Applebaum's *Twilight of Democracy: The Seductive Lure of Authoritarianism* (2020) illuminates what she describes as the shift away from democracy by elites in many nations of the world. Levitsky and Ziblatt (2019) spend more time on the US context and discuss their concern about how many US citizens feel less committed to the concepts of the rule of law and democratic institutions. These authors and many others have noted a troubling trend in the world today whereby growing numbers of people are less committed to the concept of democracy. Other research supports this observation. The American Institutional Confidence Poll (Ladd et al., 2018) reported that while 84 percent of respondents over the age of 64 agreed with the statement "Democracy is always preferable," only 55 percent of those ages 18–29 did the same. From the same data, only 11 percent of those over the age of 64 agreed with the statement "Non-democracies can be preferable" compared to 32 percent of those ages 18–29 (Ladd et al., 2018).

While these trends may not have been caused by US schools no longer teaching social studies, I fear that the effects are all connected. If we do not fight back with education for our young people, what hope do we have in a world with so many factors against us? It is only by educating all students in what it means to live in a democracy such as ours that we will survive and that our democracy will grow and thrive. This includes specific historical information about how fragile democracies can be, such as what happened to German democracy in the 1930s. It includes a deep understanding of the many rights and responsibilities that our founding documents guarantee. It includes specific information about what life is like in autocratic states and how the marketing and disinformation efforts of these nations often obscure reality. In a podcast for the Brennan Center (Boot, 2020), Applebaum shared why she wrote her book: "It's a kind of clarion call, you know, a reminder to people, don't be complacent. Democracies do fail, and in fact, all democracies in the past have failed and even most of the ones that exist now are very recent" (16:05).

An additional threat to our current system is the assault on voting rights currently underway in many parts of the nation. The situation has become so grave that a "statement of concern" was published by 100 scholars of democracy concerned about the movement to restrict the voting rights of millions of US citizens (New America, 2021). The scholars state that certain voting regulations in parts of the United States "no longer meet the minimum conditions for free and fair elections. Hence, our entire democracy is now at risk." The statement continues:

When democracy breaks down, it typically takes many years, often decades, to reverse the downward spiral. In the process, violence and corruption typically flourish, and talent and wealth flee to more stable countries, undermining national prosperity. It is not just our venerated institutions and norms that are at risk—it is our future national standing, strength, and ability to compete globally. (New America, 2021)

Students need to know their basic rights as citizens and their local and national voting rights and responsibilities. Social studies education equips students with these basics and affords them the opportunity to understand at a deeper level the meaning behind these rules and their history. Students need to learn about the brave people who worked and sacrificed for these rights. Women like Alice Paul suffered abuse and degradation for a commitment to women's suffrage. Immigrants had given up everything in their home countries to come to the United States and work toward citizenship, and that sacrifice took on important new meaning for many of them the first time they could vote. Generations of African Americans faced incredible discrimination, poll taxes, tests, and other restrictions to voting. Of all US citizens who went before us, many took great personal risks and spent huge physical effort to get to polling places to exercise their franchise.

Climate Change is a Social Studies Issue

Another major challenge for the future of our nation and our humanity involves the effects of climate change on our lives. Each of us will be affected in some way by this continuing global issue. Helping students prepare for and hopefully confront the effects of our warming atmosphere, melting ice caps, and rising seas is a huge goal that social studies education can help with. While many rightfully think about science and science education when thinking about climate change, I always include social studies as well. I believe that for answers on this issue, we need to deepen our understandings around geography, history, economics, and civics. Each of these areas has an important connection to the roots and solutions of our climate crisis. Building student comprehension and understanding of the geographic, historic, economic, and civic roots of the crisis will open their eyes to the solutions that these areas of study can offer. The practical skills needed to study and report on a topic such as the climate crisis also are an excellent opportunity to practice the investigative, analytical, and evaluation skills that social studies content teaches.

The roles of governments, economic issues, community decision making and planning, geographic realities, and so much more are natural connectors to most social studies standards and an issue that may be the most important topic that students study. In a powerful 2014 article in *Social Education*, educators Lori Kumler and Bethany Vosburg-Bluem write:

> Social studies' interdisciplinary nature provides ample opportunities for students to address potentially life-altering twenty-first century issues such as climate change. As a complex, global, and comprehensive issue, it also intersects with most of the NCSS standards and therefore can be explored in all of the social studies disciplines. Thus applying the inquiry process of the C3 Framework is a logical next step for social studies educators and students, allowing them to explore and address one of the single most impactful issues of our time. Our students are curious about the world around them, including popular media topics like climate change. Let's help them see the relevance social studies brings to their lives and futures. (p. 229)

These areas connect and serve as reasons why social studies should not continue to be an afterthought in public schools' curriculum. The purposes and practices of inquiry-based social studies instruction should be reinvigorated in every district in the United States. Teachers should be excited by the prospect of sharing their knowledge with students to help create the next cadre of citizen leaders in the United States.

This means teaching history, which is complete, complex, sometimes troubling, but always intellectually rigorous and tells the entire story of our past. This means teaching geography with a specific focus on climate change and the existential issues facing us in upcoming generations. This means teaching economics so that students understand the role of resources, labor, decision making, and power in our lives and so that they understand how their decisions can impact the future. This means teaching civics—honest, robust, messy civics—that examines the truths about the challenges in our systems while educating students about the promise of democracy and the many unique privileges our particular democratic republic offers.

CHAPTER 4

HOW WE CAN DO IT

> Democratic citizens don't grow on trees or
> appear out of thin air; rather, We The People
> must be educated. … In my judgment, this
> is why social studies is at the center, not the
> margins, of a good school curriculum and why
> it needs to begin early in the primary grades
> and continue, snowballing, straight through
> college. (Parker, 2015, p. 12)

The purpose of this book has been to present the reader
with arguments, examples, descriptions, and reasons why
social studies matters and why the recommitment to social
studies education is so necessary in our nation today. As
I conclude this plea and prayer, let me present some ideas
for what we can all do now to help this effort as well as
what I consider to be a final focus on the main reasons why
we have no choice but to share with students the critically
important gifts and tools that a sound social studies
education offers.

What can each of us do today to provide a more solid social studies education for all students?

Here are three places to start:

1. If you work with elementary students, pledge to teach some social studies every day. Support the increase of social studies instruction time in your school's schedule. Work with colleagues to actualize ways that primary and intermediate reading and English language arts instruction can work with content knowledge standards and goals to help increase student comprehension and capacity. If you work with high school students and the issue of scheduling or timing isn't the major factor (there are already defined social studies instructional time periods), pledge to make sure that the instruction provided is sequenced, inquiry and standards based, filled with diverse perspectives, and culturally relevant (Ladson-Billings, 1992). Help middle school and high school students to tackle real-life problems and see the varied connections between the study of history and their lives. Build strong, vocal, active citizens who have the skills to differentiate fact from fiction and who can demand, as well as make, evidence-based arguments about any issue.

2. Challenge districts and school leaders to invest in high-quality professional development and instructional materials that support the inquiry and standards-based goals discussed in this book. Help teachers learn the best in pedagogical practice around the teaching of social studies in the 21st century. Review and select instructional materials that support an inquiry-based methodology of teaching and include rich primary and secondary sources and diverse perspectives with a culturally relevant, antiracist, patriotic focus. Use non-commercial resources such as the Johns Hopkins Institute for Education Policy's Knowledge Maps in Reading/English Language Arts and Social Studies (edpolicy.education.jhu.edu) to help select materials that meet these challenging goals. Support efforts in every school for the highest quality broadband possible so that all students may have access to digital resources that enhance and support their learning.

3. Educate the broader community (local media, parents, grandparents, religious leaders, school boards, etc.) about the importance of high-quality, honest, inquiry-driven, historically accurate, and culturally relevant social studies instruction filled with diverse perspectives and evidence-based arguments. Advocate for the type of social studies teaching and learning that will help students become thoughtful, patriotic citizens who love their country enough to challenge inequities and work together to make ours a greater country for all its people.

What are the most important reasons to recommit to social studies education every day for every child?

Here are my top three:

1. The ever-growing influence of misinformation, disinformation, and false narratives in our nation today are propelling policy and behaviors, some violent, and are a particular threat to our coexistence, our system of government, and a peaceful future. Giving students the tools to evaluate information, understand sources, contextualize and analyze data, and sift through the plethora of information presented from a polarized set of media outlets and other sources will be key to ensuring a future that is stable, more equitable, and peaceful for all (Breakstone et al., 2021). The power and reach of artificial intelligence is growing exponentially and will impact the lives of our current primary grade students in ways we as adults can barely imagine or understand today. While we are not able to teach about things we do not understand, we can build in students the skills of critical thinking, creativity, communication, and collaboration that they will need to navigate this future. Inquiry-based social studies education provides a framework that allows all students to build up practice and efficacy in these and many other important habits of mind that will serve them well in the future, no matter the challenges that might arise.

2. An increase in high-quality, sequenced, and inquiry-based social studies education and a focus on knowledge-based reading instruction in the elementary grades can set the stage for all students to increase reading comprehension and help erode the growing "knowledge gap" between socioeconomic and racial groups (Halvorsen et al., 2012). Inequities of all sorts in our society present one of the gravest threats to a peaceful future. As any study of history shows, an increase in societal inequity is often a precursor to societal problems. Helping all students, especially those from less-advantaged groups, increases their capacity to improve reading comprehension and literacy test scores and can play a role in decreasing inequity by increasing student achievement and offering possibilities for greater opportunity to all students.

3. An increase in social studies education can help diminish the growing sense of disenfranchisement and powerlessness felt by many in the nation today. Research has shown that students who receive consistent, high-quality, effective social studies instruction are:

   • More likely to vote and discuss politics at home.
   • Four times more likely to volunteer and work on community issues.
   • More confident in their ability to speak publicly and communicate with their elected representatives. (Campaign for Civic Mission of Schools, 2011)

Given the research discussed earlier about the reduced support for democratic systems by young people and the continuing electoral success of autocratic leaders, both near and far, we must work every day to ensure that young people understand and appreciate the value of a democratic system based on the rule of law and affords all people the same rights and protections. Helping students deeply understand our history completely, with all the flaws and challenges within it, should be a goal of every district and every public school. Laws and school board policies that restrict the teaching of certain content and attempt to ban certain books as we have seen proliferate recently are a danger to our system of free and open dialogue and to the education of the young (Harris & Alter, 2022; Pollock et al., 2022). Censorship, silence, cover-up, and whitewashing do not help students better understand or appreciate this nation and its promise. We have seen these strategies used in places most Americans deride for their lack of free expression and respect for the rule of law. Teachers are already sharing concerns about the chilling effect these laws are having on classroom instruction: "She said the proposed bill makes it feel like the thought police are descending. ... She said she knows teachers who are already self-censoring. They're afraid to speak out on issues because they feel there are going to be repercussions from their districts" (Florido, 2021). An inquiry-based social studies program should not leave teachers afraid but should help them feel excited to teach the fascinating and challenging story of our nation and the world around them.

CONCLUSION

I began this work by sharing some personal insights into my education, background, and teaching experience. As a first-generation American, I have a unique perspective on the beauty and the possibility that is the United States. I know what my parents sacrificed to give my sisters and me the chance to "be American," and I am grateful to them every day. That a working-class immigrant's gay son could earn a doctorate from Harvard University might not seem that special to some, but when placed in the context of opportunity found, or denied, in many places throughout the globe, it is indeed quite extraordinary.

I also realize the profound role my race and socially conforming gender presentation have played in my life. As a white cisgender male, I have not faced the same types of challenges that people of color, women, and transgender individuals feel every day. While growing up gay with little money and foreign-born parents who had only a primary education, I still had privileges in this society that many do not. My goal as an educator has always been to help build a society that allows all students to have the opportunities they desire, regardless of identities. At the end of the day, I do believe in the promise that is the United States of America. But I know quite well and with recent history as our guide—understand deeply—that the promise is not fulfilled. The work must continue. While we have made great strides since the nation's founding, there is much more work to do. But the promise is so great, the dream so colorful and bright, that I believe the work is worth it. As educators, our role in the work is to help the next generation understand and commit to continue the effort.

Teachers do this every day in schools big and small. They touch the hearts and open the minds of students whose potential is unlimited. They are shaping the future and the nation so that one day we may all with complete honesty state the phrase and the promise: "with liberty and justice for all."

ACKNOWLEDGMENTS

I'd like to thank my colleagues at Gibbs Smith Education, especially Jeff Whorley, Jared L. Taylor, and Giacomo J. Calabria for their support, critiques, conversations, and hard work.

Thanks also to Mrs. Jean Bolgatz for reading and commenting on an early draft of the material.

Thanks, most especially, to all the educators, students, friends and colleagues I've known in my journey who have inspired and taught me so much.

And finally, to my husband, Francisco, who put up with me during the writing of this book, and who teaches me each day about the power of love.

REFERENCES

Alabama Learning Exchange. State Department of Education. (2017). Courses of study: Social studies (Grade 5). Alabama State Department of Education. https://alex.state.al.us standardAllphp?grade=5&subject=SS2010&summary=2

Applebaum, A. (2018, October). A warning from Europe: The worst is yet to come. *The Atlantic Monthly Magazine*. https://www. theatlantic.com/magazine/archive/2018/10/poland polarization/568324/

Applebaum, A. (2020). Twilight of democracy: The seductive lure of authoritarianism. Doubleday.

Baldwin, J. (1962, January 14). As much truth as one can bear. *The New York Times*. T11. https://www.nytimes.com/1962/01/14/ archives/as-much-truth-as-one-bear-to-speak-out-about-the-world-as-it-is.html

Banilower, E. R., Smith, P. S., Weiss, I. R., Malzahn, K. A., Campbell, K. M., & Weis, A. M. (2013). Report of the 2012 national survey of science and mathematics education. Horizon Research, Inc. http://www.horizon-research.com/2012nssme/wp-content/uploads/2013/02/2012-NSSME-Full-Report1.pdf

Barnum, M. (2019, April 12). Nearly a decade later, did the common core work? New research offers clues. *Chalkbeat*. https:// www.chalkbeat.org/2019/4/29/21121004/nearly-a-decade-later-did-the-common-core-work-new-research-offers-clues

Barton, K. C., & Levstik, L. S. (2004). *Teaching history for the common good*. Lawrence Erlbaum Associates.

Beal, C., & Martorella, P. H. (1994). *Social studies for elementary school classrooms: Preparing children to be global citizens*. Merrill Prentice Hall.

Beyer, B. K. (1988). *Developing a thinking skills program*. Allyn & Bacon.

Bloom, B. (1956). *A taxonomy of educational objectives. Handbook 1:*

Cognitive domain. McKay.

Boot, M. (Host). (2020, October 27). Anne Applebaum on the twilight of democracy (No. 252). [Audio podcast episode]. In *Brennan Center Live*. Brennan Center. https://www.brennancenter.org/ our-work/anaysis-opinion/podcasts/anne-applebaum-twilight-democracy

Breakstone, J., Smith, M., Wineburg, S., Rapaport, A., Carle, J., Garland, M., & Saavedra, A., (2021). Students' civic online reasoning: A national portrait. *Educational Researcher 50*(8), 505–515. https://doi.org/10.3102%2F0013189X211017495

Brophy, J., & Alleman, J. (2006). A reconceptualized rationale for elementary social studies. *Theory and Research in Social Education, 34*(4), 428–454. https://doi.org/10.1080/00933104.2 006.10473317

Bush, G. W. (2001). 9/11 address to the nation [speech]. https://www. georgewbushlibrary.gov/explore/exhibits/911-steel-american-resolve
C3 Teachers. (2015). New York State social studies resource toolkit. Is protest patriotic? https://c3teachers.org/wp-content/uploads/2015/09/NewYork_8_ Patriotism_rev.pdf

Campaign for the Civic Mission of Schools. (2011). Guardian of democracy: The civic mission of schools [report]. https://www. carnegie.org/publications/guardian-of-democracy-the-civic-mission-of-schools

Carroll, A. (Ed.). (1997). *Letters of a nation*. Broadway Books.

Center for Civic Education. (1994). Civics and government standards, K–12. https://www.civiced.org/resource-materials/national-standards-for-civics-and-government

Cheslak, C. (2018, August 30). Hedy Lamarr [biography and lesson plan]. https://www.womenshistory.org/students-and-educators/ biographies/hedy-lamarr

Chesney, B., & Citron, D. (2019). Deep fakes: A looming challenge for privacy, democracy, and national security. California Law Review. https://doi.org/10.15779/Z38RV0D15J

CIRCLE (Center for Information & Research on Civic Learning & Engagement). (2017, April 12). Millennials deeply uncertain about democracy post-election, but few believe it is in peril [report]. https://circle.tufts.edu/latest-research/millennials-deeply-uncertain-about-democracy-post-election-few-believe-it-peril

Coleman, P. T. (2022, January 6). Half the US believes another civil war is likely. Here are the 5 steps we must take to avoid that. Time Magazine. https://time.com/6133380/us-avert-civil-war/

Colleary, K. P. (2018). Student questionnaire on curriculum. Fordham Graduate School of Education course, CTGE 5061, Teaching social studies to young children [teacher files].

Council for Economic Education. (2010). Economics standards, K–12. https://www.councilforeconed.org/resources/type/standards/#sthash.l6GzfeDJ.dpbs

Cunningham, A. E., & Chen, Y. (2014). Matthew effects: The rich get richer in literacy. Encyclopedia of Language Development. SAGE Publications. https://moam.info/matthew-effects-the-rich-get-richer-in-literacy-_5a74d74d1723dd61321476ef.html

Dewey, J. (1902). *The child and the curriculum*. University of Chicago Press.

Dewey, J. (1916). *Democracy and education*. Macmillan.

Donovan, J. (2020, October 5). Thank you for posting: Smoking's lessons for regulating social media. MIT Technology Review. https://www.technologyreview.com/2020/10/05/1009231/social-media-facebook-tobacco-secondhand-smoke/

Donovan, L., Green, T. D., & Mason, C. (2014). Examining the 21st century classroom: Developing an innovation configuration map. Journal of Educational Computing Research, 50, 161–178. https://doi.org/10.2190/EC.50.2.a

Edsall, T. (2021, February 17). Democracy is weakening right in front of us. The New York Times Magazine. https://www.nytimes.com/2021/02/17/opinion/digital-revolution-democracy-fake-news.html

Educating for American Democracy. (2021). About us: Our vision. https://www.educatingforamericandemocracy.org/our-vision

Elder, L., & Paul, R. (2008). Critical thinking: The nuts and bolts of education. *Optometric Education*, 33, 88–91. https://journal. opted.org/files/Volume_33_Number_3_Summer_2008.pdf

Ennis, R. H. (1962). A concept of critical thinking: A proposed basis *for research on the teaching and evaluation of critical thinking ability. Harvard Educational Review, 32(1), 81–111.*

Evans, R. (2006). The social studies wars, now and then. *Social Education*, 70(5), 317–321. https://www.socialstudies.org/ system/files/publications/articles/se_700506317.pdf

Fitchett, P., Heafner, T., & Van Fossen, P. (2014, December). An analysis of time prioritization for social studies in elementary school classrooms. *Journal of Curriculum and Instruction*, 8(2), 7–35. https://www.researchgate.net/publication/284475326_ An_Analysis_of_Time_Prioritization_for_Social_Studies_in_ Elementary_School_Classrooms

Florido, A. (2021, May 28). Laws banning critical race theory are leading to self-censorship [radio interview]. https://www. npr.org/2021/05/28/1000537206/teachers-laws-banning-critical-race-theory-are-leading-to-self-censorship

Foundation for Critical Thinking. (2019). Our concept and definition of critical thinking. https://www.criticalthinking.org/pages/our-conception-of-critical-thinking/411

Foundation for Critical Thinking. (2022). K–12 instruction. https://www. criticalthinking.org/pages/k-12-instruction/432

Gabbatt, A. (2022, April 7). "Unparalleled in intensity"—1,500 book bans in US school districts. *The Guardian*. https://www. theguardian.com/us-news/2022/apr/07/book-bans-pen-america-school-districts

Gabriel, T., & Goldstein, D. (2021, June 1). Disputing racism's reach, Republicans rattle American schools. *The New York Times*. https://www.nytimes.com/2021/06/01/us/politics/critical-race-theory.html

Goldstein, D. (2020, January 12). Two states. Eight textbooks. Two American stories. *New York Times*. https://www.nytimes.com/interactive/2020/01/12/us/texas-vs-california-history-textbooks.html

Goldstein, D. (2022, March 18). Opponents call it the "don't say gay" bill. Here's what it says. *New York Times*. https://www.nytimes.com/2022/03/18/us/dont-say-gay-bill-florida.html

Halpern, D. F. (1998). Teaching critical thinking for transfer across domains: Disposition, skills, structure training, and metacognitive monitoring. *American Psychologist, 53*(4), 449–455. https://doi.apa.org/doiLanding?doi=10.1037%2F0003-066X.53.4.449

Halvorsen, A. L., Duke, N. K., Brugar, K. A., Block, M. K., Strachan, S. S., Berka, M. B., & Brown, J. M. (2012, May). Narrowing the achievement gap in second-grade social studies and content area literacy: The promise of a project-based approach. *Theory & Research in Social Education, 40*, 198–229. https://files.eric.ed.gov/fulltext/ED537157.pdf

Hannah-Jones, N. (2012, November 2). Soft on segregation: How the feds failed to integrate Westchester County. *Pro Publica*. https://www.propublica.org/article/soft-on-segregation-how-the-feds-failed-to-integrate-westchester-county

Harris, A. (2021, May 7). The GOP's "critical race theory" obsession. *The Atlantic Monthly Magazine*. https://www.theatlantic.com/politics/archive/2021/05/gops-critical-race-theory-fixation-explained/618828

Harris, E., & Alter, A. (2022, January 30). Book ban efforts spread across the U.S. *The New York Times*. https://www.nytimes.com/2022/01/30/books/book-ban-us-schools.html

Heafner, T. L., O'Connor, K. A., Groce, E. C., Byrd, S., Good, A. J., Oldendorf, S., Passe, J., & Rock, T. (2007). A case for advocacy: Becoming AGENTS for change. *Social Studies and the Young Learner, 20*(1), 26–27.

Heafner, T. L., & Fitchett, P. G. (2012). Tipping the scales: National trends of declining social studies instructional time in elementary schools. *Journal of Social Studies Research, 36*(2), 190–215.

Hess, F. (2021, April 13). How can educators teach students to spot fake news? *Forbes Magazine*. https://www.forbes.com/sites/

frederickhess/2021/04/13/how-can-educators-teach-students-to-spot-fake-news/

Hicks, M. (2021, August 12). Experts fear ban on critical race theory could harm civic education. *The Fulcrum*. https://thefulcrum.us/civic-ed/critical-race-theory-civic-ed

Hillocks, G., Jr. (July, 2010). EJ in Focus: Teaching argument for critical thinking and writing. *English Journal 99* (6), 24-32. https://www.jstor.org/stable/20787661

Hirsch, E. D. (1987). *Cultural literacy: What every American needs to know.* Houghton Mifflin.

Hmelo, C. E., Holton, D. L., & Kolodner, J. L. (2000). Designing learning about complex systems. *Learning Science, 9*(1), 247–298. https://doi.org/10.1207/S15327809JLS0903_2

Huijgen, T., van de Grift, W., van Boxtel, C., & Holthuis, P. (2018). Promoting historical contextualization: The development and testing of a pedagogy. *Journal of Curriculum Studies, 50*(3), 410–434. https://doi.org/10.1080/00220272.2018.1435724

Izadi, E. (2021, June 11). Darnella Frazier, the teen who filmed George Floyd's murder, awarded a Pulitzer citation. *The Washington Post*. https://www.washingtonpost.com/media/2021/06/11/darnella-frazier-pulitzer-george-floyd-witness/

Jerald, C. D. (2006, August). The hidden costs of curriculum narrowing. The Center for Comprehensive School Reform and Improvement. https://files.eric.ed.gov/fulltext/ED494088.pdf

Jordan, B. (1974). Remarks during impeachment hearings. https://millercenter.org/the-presidency/impeachment/my-faith-constitution-whole-it-complete-it-total

Kelly, K. (2016). *The inevitable: Understanding the 12 technological forces that will shape our future.* Viking.

King, M. L., Jr. (1963). I have a dream [speech]. https://www.youtube.com/watch?v=smEqnnklfYs

Kingkade, T. (2021, June 24). Uncovering who is driving the fight against critical race theory in schools [radio interview]. *Fresh Air with Terry Gross*. https://www.npr.org/2021/06/24/1009839021/uncovering-who-is-driving-the-fight-against-critical-race-theory-in-schools

Knowledge Matters Campaign. (2021). Why knowledge matters [program description]. https://knowledgematterscampaign.org/wp-content/uploads/2016/03/WhyKnowledgeMatters-1.pdf

Krahenbuhl, K. S. (2019). The problem with the expanding horizons model for history curricula. *Phi Delta Kappan, 100* (6), 20–26. https://kappanonline.org/problem-expanding-horizons-model-history-curricula-krahenbuhl/

Kuhlthau, C. C., Maniotes, L. K., & Caspari, A. K. (2007). *Guided inquiry: Learning in the 21st century.* Greenwood Publishing Group.

Kumler, L. M., & Vosburg-Bluem, B. (2014). Climate change in the social studies classroom. *Social Education, 78*(5), 225–229. https://cbexapp.noaa.gov/pluginfile.php/78140/mod_resource/content/4/Kumler%2C%20Vosburg-Bluem%20Climate%20Change%20in%20Social%20Studies.pdf

Kupers, E., Lehmann-Wermser, A., McPherson, G., & van Geert, P. (2018). Children's creativity: A theoretical framework and systematic review. *Review of Educational Research, 89*(1), 93–124. https://doi.org/10.3102/0034654318815707

Lackmeyer, S. (2021, May 30). Greenwood author's first-person history of 1921 Tulsa Race Massacre published 100 years later. *The Oklahoman.* https://www.oklahoman.com/story/news/2021/05/30/greenwood-author-publishes-black-wall-street-book-tulsa-race-massacre/5047138001/

Ladd, J. M., Tucker, J. A., & Kates, S. (2018). American institutional confidence poll: The health of American democracy in an era of hyper polarization. A report by the Baker Center for Leadership & Governance, Georgetown University, and the John S. and James L. Knight Foundation. https://www.jonathanmladd.com/uploads/5/3/6/6/5366295/2018-american-institutional-confidence-poll-1.pdf

Ladson-Billings, G. (1992). Reading between the lines and beyond the pages: A culturally relevant approach to literacy teaching. *Theory Into Practice, 31,* 312–320. https://doi.org/10.1080/00405849209543558

LeClair, C., & Gownder, J. P. (2016, June 22). The future of white-collar work: Sharing your cubicle with robots [report]. Forrester.

https://www.forrester.com/report/The-Future-Of-WhiteCollar-Work-Sharing-Your-Cubicle-With-Robots/RES132404

Levinson, M. (2007). The civic achievement gap. CIRCLE Working Paper 51. Center for Information and Research on Civic Learning and Engagement, Tufts University. http://nrs.harvard.edu/urn-3:HUL.InstRepos:10861134

Levitsky, S., & Ziblatt, D. (2019). *How democracies die*. Penguin Books.

Long, C. (2021, March 26). Fox News sued for $1.6 billion by Dominion Voting Systems for defamation [television broadcast]. PBS Newshour. https://www.pbs.org/newshour/nation/fox-news-sued-for-1-6-billion-by-dominion-voting-systems-for-defamation

Loomba, S., de Figueiredo, A., Piatek, S. J., de Graaf, K., & Larson, H. J. (2021). Measuring the impact of COVID-19 vaccine misinformation on vaccination intent in the UK and USA. *Nat Hum Behav 5*, 337–348. https://doi.org/10.1038/s41562-021-01056-1

Loveless, T. (2021). *Between the state and the schoolhouse: Understanding the failure of common core*. Harvard Education Press.

Lybarger, M. (1983). Origins of the modern social studies: 1900–1916. *History of Education Quarterly, 23*(4), 455–468. https://doi.org/10.2307/368079

Maxim, G. (1999). *Social studies and the elementary school child*. Prentice Hall.

McCance, M. (2022, March 2). How Russia's attack on Ukraine threatens democracy everywhere. *UVA Today*. https://news.virginia.edu/content/how-russias-attack-ukraine-threatens-democracy-everywhere

McCarthy, T. (23, March 2021). Pro-Trump lawyer says "no reasonable person" would believe her election lies. *The Guardian*. https://www.theguardian.com/us-news/2021/mar/23/sidney-powell-trump-election-fraud-claims

McMurren, J. (2007). *Choices, Changes, and Challenges: Curriculum and Instruction in the NCLB Era*. Center on Education Policy.

Meachem, J. (2021, July 4). State of America: A Fareed Zacharia special [video file]. https://transcripts.cnn.com/show/fzgps/date/2021-07-04/segment/01

Merton, R. K. (1968). The Matthew effect in science. *Science, 159,* 56–63. https://DOI:10.1126/science.159.3810.56

Michigan Department of Education. (2019). Social studies standards, grades K–12. https://www.michigan.gov/documents/mde/Final_Social_Studies_Standards_Document_655968_7.pdf

Marzano, R. J., Pickering, D., & Pollock, J. E. (2001). *Classroom instruction that works: Research-based strategies for increasing student achievement.* Association for Supervision and Curriculum Development.

National Center for History in the Schools. (1994). Exploring the American experience and the national standards for US History. University of California, Los Angeles. https://phi.history.ucla.edu/nchs/united-states-history-content-standards

National Center for History in the Schools. (1996). Exploring the American experience and the national standards for world history. University of California, Los Angeles. https://phi.history.ucla.edu/nchs/world-history-content-standards/

National Council for Geographic Education. (2012). Geography standards, K–12. https://ncge.org/teacher-resources/national-geography-standards/

National Council for the Social Studies. (2010). Social studies standards, K–12. https://www.socialstudies.org/standards/national-curriculum-standards-social-studies

National Council for the Social Studies. (2013). *College, career, and civic life (C3) framework for social studies state standards: Guidance for enhancing the rigor of K–12 civics, economics, geography, and history.* https://www.socialstudies.org/system/files/2022/c3-framework-for-social-studies-rev0617.2.pdf

National Governors Association Center for Best Practices, Council of Chief State School Officers. (2010). *Common core state standards English language arts* [standards]. National Governors Association Center for Best Practices, Council of Chief State School Officers. http://www.corestandards.org/ELA-Literacy

National History Day. (2021). Communication in history theme. https://
www.nhd.org/virtual2021pr/communicationinhistory

New America. (2021, June 1). Statement of concern. The threats to
American democracy and the need for national voting and
election administration standards [statement]. https://www.
newamerica.org/political-reform/statements/statement-of-
concern

Organization for Economic Co-operation and Development. (2021).
Report on social inequality. OECD Centre for Opportunity and
Equality. https://www.oecd.org/social/inequality.htm

Pace, J. (2012). Teaching literacy through social studies under No Child
Left Behind. *Journal of Social Studies Research, 36*(4), 329–358.
https://www.researchgate.net/publication/286625656_Teaching_
literacy_through_social_studies_under_No_Child_Left_Behind

Paine, T. (1776–1783). *The American Crisis.* https://www.ushistory.org/
paine/crisis

Parker, W. (Ed.). (2015). *Social studies today: Research and practice.*
Routledge.

Parker, W., & Beck, T. A. (2017). *Social studies in elementary education.*
Pearson.

Parrish, M. E. (1923/2009). *Events of the Tulsa disaster.* John Hope
Franklin Center for Reconciliation.

Partnership for 21st Century Learning. (2002). Learning and innovation
skills 4C's [framework]. Battelle for Kids. https://www.
battelleforkids.org/networks/p21/frameworks-resources

Patterson, L. (2018, June 13). The role of creativity in entrepreneurship.
Alpha Gamma. https://www.alphagamma.eu/entrepreneurship/
role-creativity-in-entrepreneurship/

Pendharker, E. (2022, January 27). Efforts to ban critical race theory now
restrict teaching for a third of America's kids. *Education Week.*
https://www.edweek.org/leadership/efforts-to-ban-critical-
race-theory-now-restrict-teaching-for-a-third-of-americas-
kids/2022/01

Pollock, M., Rogers, J., Kwako, A., Matschiner, A., Kendall, R., Bingener,
C., Reece, E., Kennedy, B., & Howard, J. (2022). The conflict

campaign: Exploring local experiences of the campaign to can "critical race theory" in public K–12 education in the U.S., 2020–2021 [report]. UCLA's Institute for Democracy, Education, and Access. https://idea.gseis.ucla. edu/publications/files/the-conflict-campaign-report

Pondiscio, R. (2014). Literacy is knowledge: Why teaching reading means teaching content. *City Journal.* https://www.city-journal.org/ html/literacy-knowledge-13623.html

Public Religion Research Institute (PRRI). (2021, May 27). Understanding QAnon's connection to American politics, religion and media consumption [report]. https://www.prri.org/ research/qanon-conspiracy-american-politics-report

Putnam, R. (2000). *Bowling alone: The collapse and revival of American community.* Simon & Schuster.

Ravitch, D. (1998). Who prepares our history teachers? Who should prepare our history teachers? *The History Teacher, 31*(4), 495–503. https://doi.org/10.2307/494312

Reagan, R. (1989). Farewell address to the nation. https://www. reaganfoundation.org/library-museum/

Reilly, R. J. (2022, January 18). The FBI's secret weapon in the Capitol attack manhunt. *Huffington Post.* https://www.huffpost.com/ entry/sedition-hunters-capitol-attack-online-sleuths-fbi-trump_n _6161da09e4b06a986bd00df1

Renken, E. (2020, April 11). *NPR* How stories connect and persuade us [radio program]. *HealthShots.* https://www.npr.org/sections/ health-shots/2020/04/11/815573198/how-stories-connect-and-persuade-us-unleashing-the-brain-power-of-narrative

Rotherham, A. J., & Willingham, D. T. (2010, Spring). "21st-century" skills: Not new, but a worthy challenge. *American Educator*, 17–20. https://www.aft.org/sites/default/files/periodicals/ RotherhamWillingham.pdf

Schmoker, M. (2020, February 1). Radical reset: The case for minimalist literacy standards. Association for Supervision and Curriculum Development. https://www.ascd.org/el/articles/radical-reset-the-case-for-minimalist-literacy-standards

Schmoker, M., & Graff, G. (2011, April 19). More argument, fewer standards. *Education Week.* https://www.edweek.org/teaching-learning/opinion-more-argument-fewer-standards/2011/04

Schwartz, O. (2018, November 12). You thought fake news was bad? Deep fakes are where truth goes to die. *The Guardian.* https://www.theguardian.com/technology/2018/nov/12/deep-fakes-fake-news-truth

Schwartz, S. (2021, August 21). Who decides what history we teach? An explainer. *Education Week.* https://www.edweek.org/teaching-learning/who-decides-what-history-we-teach-an-explainer/2021/08

Shanahan, T., & Shanahan, C. (2012). What is disciplinary literacy and why does it matter? *Topics in Language Disorders, 32*(1), 7–18. https://doi:10.1097/TLD.0b013e318244557a

Shepherd, H. G. (1998, September). The probe method: A problem-based learning model's effect on critical thinking skills of fourth- and fifth-grade social studies students. *Dissertation Abstracts International, Section A: Humanities and Social Sciences, 59*(3-A), 0779.

Smith, T. (2022, January 4). Why is the "big lie" proving so hard to dispel? [radio program]. *All Things Considered.* https://www.npr.org/2022/01/04/1070337968/why-is-the-big-lie-proving-so-hard-to-dispel

Snyder, T. (2021, June 29). The war on history is a war on democracy. The New York Times Magazine. https://www.nytimes.com/2021/06/29/magazine/memory-laws.html

Stout, C., & Wilburn, T. (2022, February 1). CRT map: Efforts to restrict teaching racism and bias have multiplied across the US. *Chalkbeat.* https://www.chalkbeat.org/22525983/map-critical-race-theory-legislation-teaching-racism

Strack, R., Carrasco, M., Kolo, P., Nouri, N., Priddis, M., & George, R. (2021, March 18). The future of jobs in the era of AI [report]. *The Network.* Boston Consulting Group. https://www.bcg.com/publications/2021/impact-of-new-technologies-on-jobs

Sumner, W. G. (1906). *Folkways: A study of the sociological importance of usages, manners, customs, mores, and morals.* Ginn and Co.

Swan, K., Lee, J., & Grant, S. G. (2018). *Inquiry design model: Building inquiries in social studies.* National Council for the Social

Studies (NCSS).

Tyner, A., & Kabourek, S., (2020, September 24). Social studies instruction and reading comprehension: Evidence from the early childhood longitudinal study [report]. Thomas B. Fordham Institute. https://fordhaminstitute.org/national/resources/social-studies-instruction-and-reading-comprehension

Uerling, D., & O'Reilly, R. (1989). Local control of education. *Lincoln Publications of Center for Public Affairs Research (UNO)*. University of Nebraska–Lincoln. https://digitalcommons.unl.edu/cgi/viewcontent.cgi?article=1031&context=cpar

US Department of Education. (2021). Education in a pandemic: The disparate impacts of COVID-19 on America's students [report]. https://www2.ed.gov/about/offices/list/ocr/docs/20210608-impacts-of-covid19.pdf

VanFossen, P. (2005). "Reading and math take so much of the time…" An overview of social studies instruction in elementary classrooms in Indiana. *Theory and Research in Social Education, 33*(3), 376–403. https://doi.org/10.1080/00933104.2005.10473287

Wade, R. (2002). Beyond expanding horizons: New curriculum development directions for elementary social studies. *The Elementary School Journal, 103*(2), 115–130. https://doi.org/10.1086/499719

Walberg, H. J., & Tsai, S. L. (1983). Matthew effects in education. *American Educational Research Journal, 20*(3), 359–373. https://www.researchgate.net/profile/Herbert-Walberg/publication/250184530_%27Matthew%27_Effects_in_Education/links/542011d70cf2218008d43991/Matthew-Effects-in-Education.pdf

Walsh, C. (2020, August 28). Why some Americans refuse to social distance and wear masks: Michael Sandel explores the ethics of what we owe each other in a pandemic [interview]. *The Harvard Gazette*. https://news.harvard.edu/gazette/story/2020/08/sandel-explores-ethics-of-what-we-owe-each-other-in-a-pandemic/

Walter, B. F. (2022). *How civil wars start and how to stop them*. Crown.

Warder, G. (2015). Horace Mann and the creation of the Common School. *Social Welfare History Project* [website]. http://www.disabilitymuseum.org/dhm/edu/essay.html?id=42